AF471637

ISBN 978-1-304-84496-5

STILL MARRIED...

...STILL LAUGHING

Janice Schwartz-Wasserman

DEDICATION

This is dedicated to the one I love.

INTRODUCTION

Take a Latina from the Midwest and a Jew from the Bronx and what do you get.....hilarity! This is what I work with eight hours a day, five days a week (except snow days). Seriously, I am working with a woman who is as funny (can't say funnier) as my husband. I am greeted each morning with "Hi Hoe". I have been called slut, tramp, and loser....daily. Her new one is Wasserhoe". Now that's creative. I have gotten so used to it I don't even respond. Once in a while when she calls me loser, I remind her that I am the one with the college degree.

Sharing an office with her is never dull. Actually it's quite scary. For some unknown reason she thinks I adore clowns and monkeys (very ugly monkeys) so she's covered my shelves, walls and computer with them. She enjoys telling our students that they are my babies! Those poor kids get so confused.

Not caring is her mantra. When something terrible happens to me and I go to her for consoling, she cuts me off midstream and replies, "I don't care". Most of the time she doesn't even give me a chance to tell her what happened because she starts laughing uncontrollably. I get no sympathy.

My birthday is the scariest day of all for me at work. She likes to steal my car keys and move it so I think it's stolen. I got wise after the first two years. But its what she puts in my car that is, well, disturbing. Like a pink thong on my steering wheel, condoms on the seats, a deck of cards with naked men strewn all over, huge posters of porn scenes with pictures of MY face glued over the "actresses", balloons packed to the roof and Happy Birthday painted all over. Needless to say, driving home on those days, I'm very careful not to exceed the speed limit.

I remember one time asking her how her Dad's back was doing. She told me he was not taking any meds for the pain. So I asked her what he was doing. She answered, "My Mother!"

How lucky I am to work with this wacky woman and then come home to my hilarious man. Whether its spouses, friends, relatives or colleagues, that make you laugh, humor is what makes our lives tolerable, endurable and hopefully enjoyable. (and it's cheaper than therapy!). Enjoy!

Chapter 1

LIFE LESSONS (WHY MEDITATE WHEN YOU CAN MEDICATE)

Sadly, our dog got old,
so I told my husband,
“We need to put him down.
He said,
“Let’s just drop him off
in a Korean neighborhood
– it’s cheaper!”

I asked a teacher at work if she thought
we would have a snow day tomorrow.
She said, “Nah, we’re only getting two
to three inches tonight
– that’s not enough to get off.”
You’re telling me!

My daughter is dating a medical
student who is Greek.
I guess when the relatives ask me if he's Jewish,
I can say, "Well, he's Orthodox!"

The worst question you could ask a Guy,
"Is it in yet?"

A colleague at work said,
"Things have gotten so bad
they put a Prozac lick in the teacher's lounge!"

We bought a summer place in the town
we used to go camping back in the seventies.
It's weird having sex in a house instead of a tent.
And wait…where's the Qualudes?
And why are we wearing clothes?

Leave it to my dog to get heartworms
on Valentine's Day!

Our hydrangeas remind me
of our college buddy Sheldon…
...they both like acid!

My husband challenged me with,
"I bet you can't say something to piss me
off and make me happy all at the same time".
I thought for a second than replied, "Yes I can.
Your brother has a smaller dick than you do!"

I was complaining to him how I wanted an eye job
because that extra skin makes me look so old.
He said, "I had some skin removed...
...about sixty years ago!"

Since I got Botox, the only thing tight on me
is my forehead!

My man's Rolex stopped working.
He found out it winds automatically
with hand movement,
so now he jerks off twice a day!
(Break for me).

I tell my friends – at our age,
it's not about a lotta love,
it's about ... a lotta lube!

I went for an eye exam because
my readers were just not cutting it anymore.
The receptionist asked me if I tried a higher power.
I said sure, "I prayed and prayed
but I'm still not seeing any better!"

What have I learned from having knee surgery?
That Percoset is on MY food pyramid (wish I had a third leg!)

On Sunday morning
I asked my man
what he was making me for breakfast.
He said "Happy!"
I won't argue with that.

I realized that I don't need a facelift after all.
I just need to get my neck lowered!

He got a new hobby- composting.
Nothing like having a bowl of garbage
sitting on your kitchen counter.
However, I must admit it does work.
Last summer our hydrangeas were huge!
So now he's putting that crap down his pants!

I bought a mood ring at a head shop last summer
but I forgot what the colors mean.
My gay friend, Barry, told me blue means I'm ovulating
and a fourth grader told me blue means I'm sad.
So I guess I'm ovulating AND I'm depressed?

I've decided that exercise is like a virgin
– it's hard to squeeze it in.

On a recent road trip,
we stayed at a Super 8
(the man is cheap what can I say).
However, the sex was great
because I splurged and got the stimulus package!

If they want priests to stop having sex,
why don't they let them get married?

The best part of having kids is that they leave.
Empty nest: bong out and clothes off!
Wahoo!!!

Weekends are just like dicks- never long enough!

After my knee surgery, my doctor said
I can drive as long as I know that
I can brake if a child runs in front of my car.
I told him that's not a problem
since I don't brake for kids.
Animals sometimes. Dogs yes, squirrels
– depends on my mood
(or how hungry I am- hey I used to live in Mississippi).
So I asked my husband to dart in front of my car to see
if I can stop.
He wouldn't do it.

I got pink eye from a student.
My man didn't care.
All he said was he only wants one thing
that's pink and it's not my eye.

I bought a three pack of hoop earrings
at the Dollar Store.
I can't decide if I AM cheap
or if I'm just going to LOOK cheap.

Our friends are planning a wedding
– barefoot in the park.
They say they only want homemade gifts
so my husband started building a grow room!

We had to call the police
because some guy was threatening us.
The police office said,
"This guy has two arrests for battery."
What does my husband tell the cop?
"No wonder he was so charged up!"

What do you call it when you wish you had some weed?
High hopes!

Driving through Amish country,
we saw a man riding a motorized bicycle.
I said I thought they aren't allowed to use electricity.
My man explained,
"No motor - there's a tiny horse inside
– it's a one horse powered vehicle!"

Moving into our new house,
we wondered why the movers
were giving us weird looks.
Then we saw the boxes they were moving
into our kid's rooms.
They were labeled "S & M BEDROOM".
(Our kid's names are Susie and Michael!)

Kids say the "cutest "things.
A while back, my daughter needed to have blood drawn.
Waiting for the doctor to come in, she asked me,
"Can't I just give him a used tampon?"

Chapter 2

WHILE YOU'RE DOWN THERE

You know you had a good night when
you wake up the next morning
with a hair in your mouth...
...and it's not yours!

My man is such a pain in the ass.
He says he wants to go where no man has gone before.
How many times do I have to tell him – "Exit Only!"

I told him not to eat the meat in the refridge
because it's old.
He said, "You're old and I eat you!" Geez!

When he made muffins the other morning,
I asked him what flavor they were.
He grabbed his crotch and said, "Banana nut!"
So mature.

Let's see. Is sex all he thinks about?
Before he puts hardboiled eggs in the refridge,
he writes on them, "Eat me-I'm hard!

When I told my husband I wanted to learn fly fishing,
he wasted no time unzipping his pants. "Here ya go!"
So accommodating.

I was having stomach problems
so the doctor said I needed an endoscopy.
I told him no tube goes down my throat
unless it's attached to a really cute guy!

My man was getting frisky the other morning,
so I told him, "No, I have a sore throat".
He said, "I'll just put some chloraseptic on the tip!"
He should have been a doctor!

We had a chili luncheon at work the other day.
The meat was too greasy so I told them
I always drain my meat first.
Those crazy teachers called my husband
to see if I was lying!

The other night I was feeling nauseous and dizzy
so he said, "Bend over and put your head
between your legs.
If that doesn't help, bend over and put your head
between MY legs!"

While shopping at Party City,
I said, "Isn't this the best place to come?"
Pointing to my mouth, he said, "No, THIS is!"

My man must think he's Zorro.
When he comes, he write his initials across my chest!

He wanted to know why I needed to eat something
before we went out to brunch.
I said, "You know I have low blood sugar
-do you want me to start shaking?"
He replied, "Depends on what you're holding!"

My friend is so frigid,
the only thing she'll go down on
is an escalator!

Whenever I blow my nose
he yells, "I'm next!"

While in bed,
I asked him to bring me the moisturizer.
He grabbed his crotch and said,
"It's right here in my pants, self-service, hand pump, lip-activated!"
(I must say it's cheaper than Lubriderm).

He was having stomach issues
so, I told him that eating ginger
is very good for that.
He said ,"Great, give me her number!"

I was on the phone scheduling a colonoscopy
when I heard him yell out, "When do I get in?"

Recovering from foot surgery,
I told him how it's going to be
hard to get my pants off.
He said, "Well, if I do it then it's REALLY
going to be hard!"
Come on – I just had surgery.

Chapter 3

WOMEN-THE OTHER PINK MEAT

After we left my friend's condo,
I was telling my husband
what good taste she has in decorating.
He said "I don't want a woman with good taste,
I want a woman that tastes good!"

I was gone for part of the summer,
so I told my man that when I miss him
I just put my nose up to his bottle of cologne.
He said, "Oh yeah, when I miss you
I just smell some tilapia!"

For Fathers Day.
I asked him if he wanted breakfast in bed.
He said, "Sure, sit on my face!"

I ran into my friend Shelly at
Dick's Sporting Goods the other day.
She told me she was shopping for a new bicycle.
I said , "Let me get this straight.
You're in a store called Dick's looking for something
you can put between your legs to ride on"?

He gave me a kiss right after
I had eaten a tuna sandwich.
He said "Ooh, fishy at both ends!"

I told him to drink cherry juice
because it's good for his gout.
He said, "Perfect, the babysitter's coming over tonight!"

When rolling joints,
my husband said, he likes his joints
like he likes his women...tight!

My neighbor can get a lil dirty at times.
He told us his brother is dating an Asian girl.
He said he gets to eat Chinese every night.
My husband chimed in with,
"And I bet an hour later he wants more!"

I was on meds for a urinary tract infection
so I called the pharmacist to ask if I can have sex.
He said "Sure, I go on break in five minutes!"

I was talking about a friend the other day
and he said that it's not nice to gossip.
I said, "yeah you're right, loose lips sink ships."
He said, "Oh no, that just means it goes in easier!"

I love when he calls me at
the end of a workday and says,
"Slide down the bannister
and warm up dinner Honey,
I'm coming home!"

He had a sore neck and the doctor
said he needed moist heat
so he asked me to wrap my legs around his head.
What?

Soon as I got home from work he started groping me.
I told him I had a yeast infection
(I figured that would stop him).
His reply, "Cool, it'll rise when I put it in!"

His head was in the refridge smelling the milk
so I asked him if he smelled everything before he ate it.
He said, "No, just milk and pussy!"

My husband wears a t-shirt that says
"I'm not a gynecologist but I can take a look!"
Really?

My husband and I were heading out for a party
and as soon as we got in the car I whipped out the CDs
and asked him what he wanted to hear.
He said, "My balls slapping against your ass!"
Does he EVER think about anything else?

Chapter 4

SERIOUSLY?

The students handed out candy for Halloween
but I wouldn't eat it because it's from Mexico
(probably full of lead).
I told my para, I don't want to get retarded.
She said, "Well, that ship has sailed!"

The dinner I cooked last night was so gentile,
he said that his foreskin grew back!

I was dealing with a bladder infection
and the principal would not let me leave
the meeting to go to the bathroom.
I said to him, "Who do you think I am
...Urethra Franklin?"
(He didn't laugh.)

I was watching the Food Network
and my man overheard "creamy, salty, nutty".
He thought it was a show about him.
(He always thinks it's about him).

My friend explained to me the drug test
he created for his new business.
He lays out three piles of pot
and asks potential hires to
identify their country of origin.
You must get all three right.
ZERO TOLERANCE.
Where do I sign up?

If I knew gravity was gonna do this to my face,
I would have stood on my head the first forty years!

We were having dinner in a small town
and our waiter was gay,
I said to my husband, "What does a gay guy
do in a town like this?"
He replied, "suck a lotta dick!"
I know I can always count on him for an answer.

I was shopping at Dick's Sporting Goods
so I asked my friend if he needed anything.
He said, "Nah, I shop at Vagina's!"

My husband thought Palm Sunday
was the day men jerk off!
He needs to get out more!
(He prefers Ass Wednesday).

My friend hasn't had a date in so long,
she carries a Koran with her when she flies!

My niece's son had to have that surgery
where they drop the testicles.
So my genius husband thought
they should have done it on New Year's Eve!

It was hot in the house so I yelled down,
"What's the thermostat on?"
He said, "The wall!"
Such a wiseass!

My friend in California is concerned
about the overpopulation of stray dogs.
My husband's suggestion
– increase the Korean population!

My favorite type of donut – Ovarian Cream.
You know, the ones that come in your mouth.
Oh, I mean Bavarian Cream.

He gets gas whenever he eats Mexican food.
Now he's was wondering if our friend Jose
has the same problem when he eats his wife!

Our gay friend is so flaming
we think he farts show tunes!

The other day my man said women are like fish
– they should be battered and fried. Lil scary.

When we stayed in Vegas,
our room had a mirror on the ceiling over the bed.
My husband asked me,
"Did you see the sign on the mirror?"
"Caution: Objects in mirror
may be larger than they appear!"
Yikes!

My friend the podiatrist is putting
his wife through med school.
She's gonna be a gynecologist.
He wants to share a practice with her
so he can call it "PUSS N BOOTS!"

As we pulled into our driveway late one afternoon,
we told our son the grass needed cutting,
The poor kid was tired so my husband said,
"Just mow half ... THE TOP HALF!"

Chapter 5

MY MAN THE LEXICOLOGIST

Because we got frisky on the first night of Chanukah, he now calls me his "Menorahorah!"

I was telling him about my friend's boob job. He called it "A Tale of Two Titties!"

Connectile Dysfunction
– no cell service in the mountains.

I told my husband that our principal
said she is not having a holiday party this year.
So he whipped out his schlong and said,
"Staff party right here!"

What do you call a person from Asia who is gay?
Gaysian!

Last night I told him I was
in the mood for Chinese food,
so he said, "I'll eat your egg hole, you eat my wang,
then I won't have to wok off by myself!"

My husband is on this new diet ... he is now officially a ... VAGITARIAN!

The other day he told me,
"If you won't lick my balls,
there's a service I can call that will
... LICKAMAIDS!"

What do you call a duck that's having an orgasm?
PEKING!

So now he thinks he's Australian.
The other night he asked me if I wanted
out back or down under?

Back in High School,
my boyfriend worked
at a gas station.
He pumped gas by day
and humped ass by night!

My husband found a new TV show
on the Food channel.
He thinks it's about one of my trampy friends
because it's called,
"Mexican Made Easy."

Most people have high expectations.
My husband has expectations to get high!

Last weekend his back went out
so I had to mow the lawn.
Now he calls me his MOWHO!

I was in a grumpy mood
because I had a yeast infection.
So what does he call me ...
"The Wicked Witch of the Yeast!"

Monica Lewinsky – a Jewmador!

We were watching a movie
where the guy used a whoopee cushion
for sound effects,
So my man farted and said,
"See, I can do Foley through my holey!"
Such a classy guy.

I tried to teach him Pilates thinking maybe,
just maybe, he will get into shape.
Now he calls me his COREWHORE!

He wants me to have one of those vaginal "face" lifts.
He calls it a "FUCK TUCK!"

I told my husband that our friend's daughter
was studying to be a Doola.
It's a massage therapist for pregnant women.
He said if she gets a job in Hawaii,
then she'll be a HOOLADOOLA!"
(He's always thinking)

My husband thinks he's an inventor.
He puts toothpaste on my boobs
so he can brush his teeth
and have fun at the same time.
He calls it "BREASTCREST!"

What do you call a retarded Indian?
NATIVE VEGITATION!

We went for a run together but
I had to stop because I got a leg spasm.
He called it a "BITCH TWITCH!" Such a caring man!

I just signed up for a Jewish exercise class.
My husband calls it, "STRETCH-N-KVETCH!"

Entomology according to my man:
adult gay flies are fruit flies
and the babies are called ... faggots!"

As I was putting on makeup the other night,
he yelled out, "I don't want LIPSTICK
on my DIPSTICK!"

He loves to Salsa. He calls it "FLOORPLAY!"

We were taking a road trip and I said,
"Look at all the cows laying down in the field".
He said, "Oh, that's GROUND BEEF!"

In the morning he gets up after breakfast
and announces,
"Running late-gotta dump n dash!"
Why are men so disgusting?
(draining the lizard isn't much better).

He wants to know if people
drink chi tea while doing TAI CHI.
He needs to get a life!

He tells me he has a rectal problem ... me.
I'm a pain in his ASS!

Chapter 6

THE ANSWER: SQUARE FOOTAGE THE QUESTION: WHAT'S THE SECRET TO AN ENDURING, I MEAN HAPPY MARRIAGE?

I was explaining to my husband that
I found out I have morning duty at school this year.
He said, "Me too. As a matter of fact,
I have it every morning.
I'm so regular, you can set your clock to my colon!"
Eew!

He was so sick of my talking,
he took me to a silent auction!

He loves munching on nuts when he's watching TV.
That's when I leave the room.
The sound he makes while eating them
makes me want to kill!
And he always gives me the same answer:
"I'll stop eating nuts when you start eating mine!"
Not funny, not even normal.

I was not happy that we missed
the air show last weekend.
So he went around the house farting all day!
Always trying to please me.

He thought the SAG Awards was a show at my boobs!

I told him my BFF is looking for a soul mate.
He said he's just looking for a hole mate!
Such a romantic.

We were getting ready for a
wedding and I asked him, “Am I overdressed?”
He said, “Yeah, take off your panties !”

I told him that I read happiness is an inside job.
He said, “Yep, when it’s inside, I’m happy!”
I’m confused.

When The Good Wife is on TV,
he yells out "Take notes!"

When he picked me up from the airport,
I told him the air on the plane was so dry,
I felt it in my eyes.
He said, "You want me to lick em?"
Ah yes, always ready with that tongue.

We were in a store during Easter time
and he turned to me and said,
"Want me to buy you some new eggs?"
Gee, that made me feel young!

My husband told me that my sex drive is in PARK!

Nothing like domestic life with my man.
The other day I told him the wash needed to be folded.
His reply, “Yeah, well my dick needs to be sucked!”
So helpful.

I told my husband that I was tired
so I was going to lie down and do nothing.
He said “Oh, ya mean we’re gonna have sex?”

People ask us why we don’t take the dog
with us to NY for the summer.
He tells them, “We only have room
in the car for one bitch.
Maybe next year we’ll take the dog!”

My husband says I remind him of mozzarella cheese
– LOW MOISTURE!

We were going out for the evening
and I told him I'm not going to change.
His reply, "Oh, so you're gonna STAY a bitch?"

We were at the dog park and
I told him I needed to use the bathroom
and I didn't want to use the port-a-potty.
So he said, "Why don't you just squat
like the other bitches?"

We were meeting at an art gallery after work.
I told him I'll be a little late because
I want to look really good.
His reply, "How will I recognize you?"
And people wonder why I have no self-esteem.

Whenever I do downward facing dog,
he becomes the pokey little puppy!

ABOUT THE AUTHOR

Even though my middle name is Penny, my brothers would tease me by calling me Penelope (this was in addition to telling me that I was adopted). At night (we all shared the same bedroom), they would have spitting fights. I'll never forget the time they got me right between the eyes! And those are my good memories!

After getting married at twenty-one, I got int the habit of following my husband around th country. I have lived in four states in forty years of marriage. To my disappointment, I discovered there are no awards for this. When people ask me how I ended up in Kansas, I always give the same reply "Wrong plane!"

Along the way I picked up a Master of Education degree and who knows what from my husband. I say this because whenever he would return from a business trip overseas, I would ask him if he picked anything up for me. He always gave me the same answer. He's scratch his crotch and say, "I don't think so!" I never knew whether to laugh or get a penicillin shot!

Born and raised in the Bronx, I live in Kansas City with my husband who... ...still keeps me laughing.

www.ingramcontent.com/pod-product-compliance
Ingram Content Group UK Ltd.
Pitfield, Milton Keynes, MK11 3LW, UK
UKHW041924190726
13854UKWH00003B/1427

9 781304 844965